THE GREAT PICTURE HUNT

HEY, WALLY FANS, WELCOME TO THE GREAT PICTURE HUNT – IT'S MORE THAN A BOOK, IT'S AN ART ADVENTURE!

THE FUN STARTS OVER THE PAGE, IN EXHIBIT 1, ODLAW'S PICTURE PANDEMONIUM, WHERE YOU'LL FIND 30 ENORMOUS PORTRAITS. WOW! AMAZING! EXAMINE THEM CAREFULLY, PICTURE PERUSERS, BECAUSE EVERY ONE OF THE PORTRAIT SUBJECTS CAN BE FOUND SOMEWHERE ELSE IN THIS BOOK.

OUR QUEST BEGINS AT EXHIBIT 1 AND ENDS AT EXHIBIT 11, PIRATE PANORAMA. SOMEWHERE IN THESE ELEVEN SCENES THE 30 CHARACTERS WILL APPEAR ... BUT ONLY ONCE! YOUR CHALLENGE IS TO FIND THESE SLIPPERY SUBJECTS WHEREVER THEY MAY BE HIDING.

BUT THE FUN DOESN'T STOP THERE. LOOK OUT FOR THE SPOT-THE-DIFFERENCE PUZZLES, MATCHING GAMES, AND THE CHALLENGING CHECKLISTS WITH MORE THINGS TO SPOT FOR EXTRA WALLY-WATCHING CREDIT. FANTASTIC!

AND NOW, GALLERY GAZERS, HAVE FUN, DON'T MAKE AN EXHIBITION OF YOURSELVES, AND LET THE GREAT PICTURE HUNT BEGIN!

Wally

AND, OF COURSE, OUR PORTRAIT GAME APART, THERE ARE FIVE INTREPID PORTRAITEERS TO FIND IN EVERY SCENE...

FIND WALLY ... OUR YOUNG GALLERY GUIDE, WHO TRAVELS EVERYWHERE!
FIND WOOF ... WHO WAGS HIS NOT-SO-BRUSH-LIKE TAIL (WHICH IS ALL YOU CAN SEE!).
FIND WENDA ... WHO TAKES THE PICTURES (BUT DOESN'T PAINT THEM!).
FIND WIZARD WHITEBEARD ... THE OLD MASTER WHO CASTS COLOURFUL SPELLS!
FIND ODLAW ... WHO'S BEEN AN EXHIBIT IN MANY A ROGUES' GALLERY!

AND NOT FORGETTING MY LOST KEY, WENDA'S MISPLACED CAMERA, WOOF'S MISSING BONE, WIZARD WHITEBEARD'S MISLAID SCROLL AND ODLAW'S ABSENT BINOCULARS...

EXHIBIT 1 – ODLAW'S PICTURE PANDEMONIUM

WOW, WALLY FANS, WHAT A PANDEMONIUM! HAVE YOU EVER SEEN SO MANY YELLOW-AND-BLACK STRIPES IN ONE PLACE? AMAZING! WE'RE HERE IN ODLAW'S PICTURE GALLERY AND JUST LOOK AT WHAT HIS ARTFUL ASSOCIATES HAVE BROUGHT WITH THEM – 30 PECULIAR PORTRAITS IN AN ODDITY OF FRAMES. AMAZING! THERE'S QUITE A CAST OF CHARACTERS IN THESE PAINTINGS, AND THEY ALL APPEAR AGAIN ELSEWHERE IN THE BOOK. AND PICTURE THIS – ONE OF THEM EVEN APPEARS SOMEWHERE IN THIS CRAZY CROWD! SO PATIENTLY PERUSE THE PICTURE UNTIL YOU FIND HIM. GOOD LUCK WHEREVER YOU LOOK IN YOUR HUNT FOR THE PLACES WITH THE FACES! WHAT A PICTURE!

EXHIBIT 2 —
A SPORTING LIFE

WELCOME, PICTURE HUNT PALS, TO MY
SPECIAL REPORT FROM THE LAND OF
SPORT. FANTASTIC! IT'S LIKE THE OLYMPICS
EVERY DAY HERE, BUT WITH SO MANY ATHLETIC
EVENTS ON THE MENU THERE'S NO TIME LEFT
FOR ANY REST AND RELAXATION. HOWEVER
THERE'S NOTHING TOO STRENUOUS ABOUT
OUR MAIN EVENT, THE GREAT PICTURE
HUNT, SO KEEP YOUR EYES ON THE BALL
AND HAVE YOUR POINTER FINGERS
READY. ON YOUR MARKS,
GET SET, GO!

EXHIBIT 5 – THE PINK PARADISE PARTY

IT'S SATURDAY NIGHT, THE TEMPERATURE IS RISING AND IT LOOKS AS IF A RASH OF MUSICAL MAYHEM AND DISCO FEVER HAS BROKEN OUT IN THIS DIZZY DANCE HALL. WOW! AMAZING! HIP HIP-HOPPERS, BODY-POPPERS, ROCK-AND-ROLLERS AND BODY-AND-SOULERS – IT'S A PACKED-OUT, PARTYGOERS' PINK PARADISE. SO GET ON DOWN, CUT YOUR GROOVE AND MAKE YOUR MOVES – IT'S TIME TO SHUFFLE YOUR FEET TO THE PICTURE HUNT BEAT!

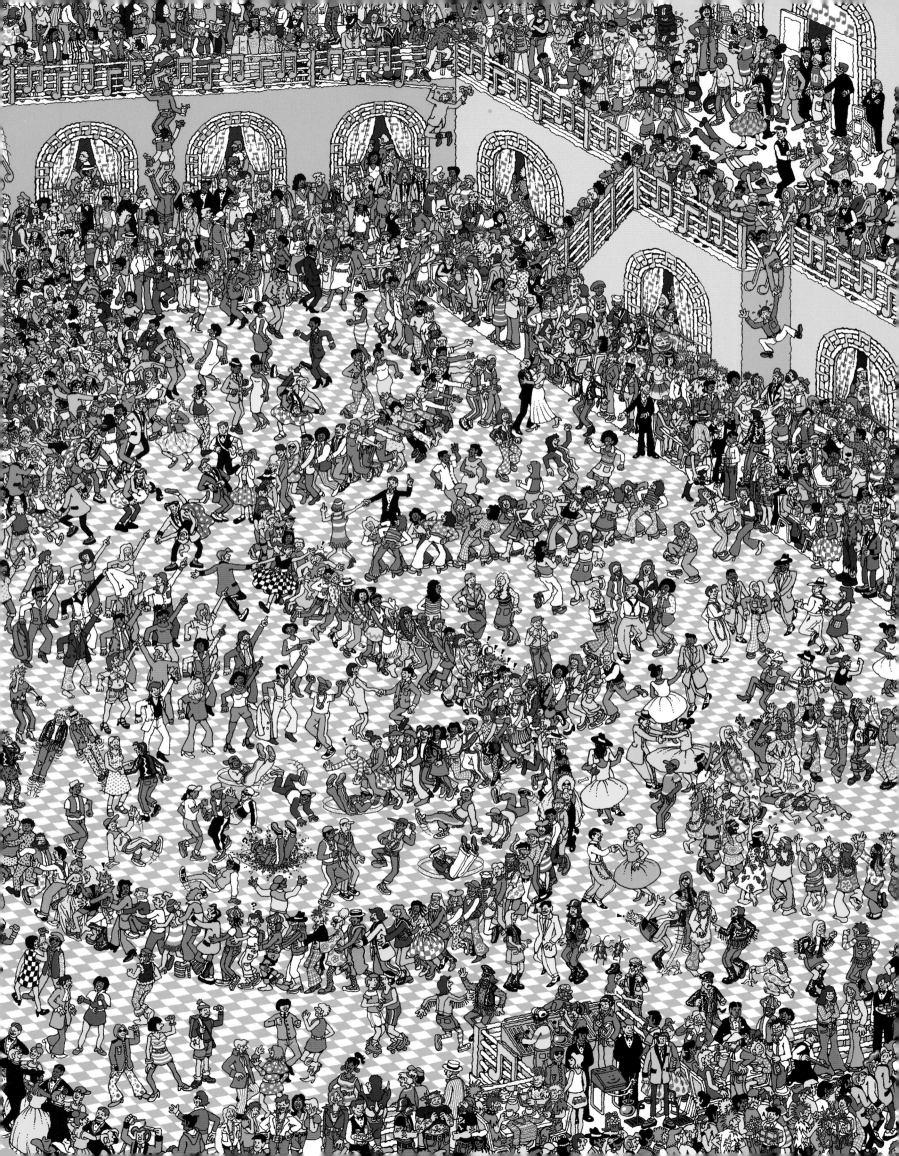

EXHIBIT 6 – OLD FRIENDS

AH, PICTURE HUNT PALS, HOW I LOVE TO LOOK THROUGH MY SCRAPBOOKS OF MEMORIES AND SOUVENIRS. THIS PAGE IS ONE OF MY FAVOURITES: A COLLAGE CRAMMED WITH FAMILIAR FACES FROM MY EARLIER ADVENTURES. FANTASTIC! EVEN THE MOST DEDICATED OF WALLY WATCHERS AMONGST YOU WILL HAVE TROUBLE RECOGNIZING ALL OF THE OLD FRIENDS HERE, IT'S QUITE A CHALLENGE. BUT HERE'S AN EASIER TEASER THAT ANYONE CAN DO: JUST LOOK AT ALL THE CIRCLED FACES IN THIS FRAME, THEN SEE IF YOU CAN SPOT THEM IN THE SURROUNDING PICTURE.

EXHIBIT 7 – OLD FRIENDS AGAIN

IT'S ALWAYS NICE WHEN FRIENDS CAN STAY FOR A LITTLE LONGER... I'VE CALLED THIS "OLD FRIENDS AGAIN" BECAUSE THAT'S EXACTLY WHAT IT IS ... A FRAMED COLLECTION OF SOME OF THE OLD FRIENDS FROM THE PICTURE NEXT DOOR, BUT IN SILHOUETTE FORM. AND JUST TO MAKE IT A BIT MORE INTERESTING, SOME OF THEM ARE PICTURED UPSIDE DOWN OR SIDEWAYS. CAN YOU MATCH EACH SILHOUETTE HERE WITH THE CORRECT OLD FRIEND IN EXHIBIT 6? SO, ONWARDS AND UPWARDS (AND DOWNWARDS AND SIDEWAYS), PICTURE HUNT PORTRAITEERS!

EXHIBIT 9 – WALLYWORLD

WOW! WHAT A HOOPY, LOOPY WORLD WE'RE IN, GALLERY GAZERS – NOT JUST A WORLD OF WALLIES, BUT A WORLD OF WHITEBEARDS, WENDAS, WOOFS AND AN ODDITY OF ODLAWS AS WELL. AMAZING! BUT LOOK AGAIN... THERE'S ONLY ONE REAL WALLY HERE, AND THE SAME GOES FOR MY FRIENDS, TOO. DON'T FORGET THAT YOU CAN ONLY TELL IF WE'RE THE GENUINE ARTICLES BY CHECKING EVERYTHING – FROM OUR GLASSES TO OUR STRIPES. CAST YOUR EYES ACROSS THESE LINES OF LOOKALIKES AND SEE IF YOU CAN FIND US!

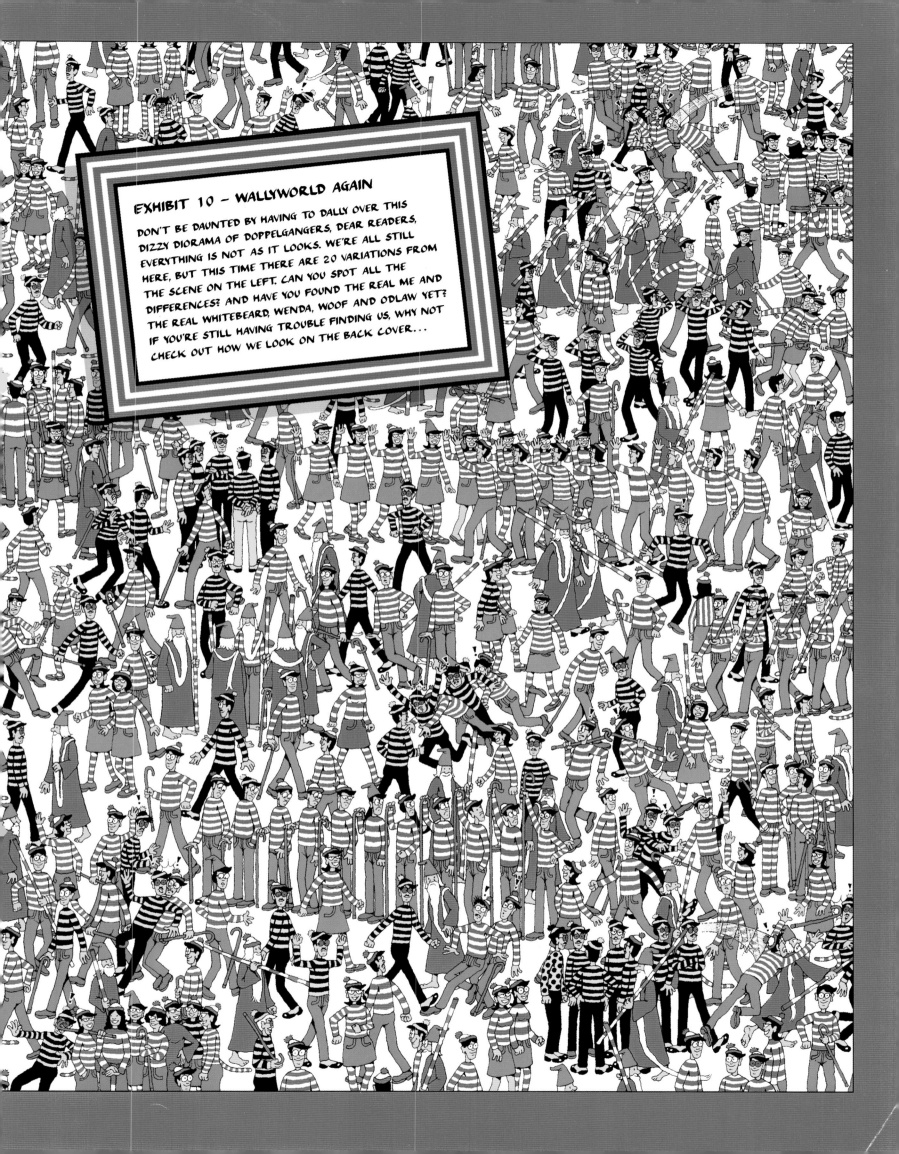

EXHIBIT 10 – WALLYWORLD AGAIN

DON'T BE DAUNTED BY HAVING TO DALLY OVER THIS DIZZY DIORAMA OF DOPPELGANGERS, DEAR READERS, EVERYTHING IS NOT AS IT LOOKS. WE'RE ALL STILL HERE, BUT THIS TIME THERE ARE 20 VARIATIONS FROM THE SCENE ON THE LEFT. CAN YOU SPOT ALL THE DIFFERENCES? AND HAVE YOU FOUND THE REAL ME AND THE REAL WHITEBEARD, WENDA, WOOF AND ODLAW YET? IF YOU'RE STILL HAVING TROUBLE FINDING US, WHY NOT CHECK OUT HOW WE LOOK ON THE BACK COVER...

EXHIBIT 11 – PIRATE PANORAMA

SHIVER ME TIMBERS, SHIPMATES, WHAT PERFIDIOUS, PIRATE PANORAMA IS THIS? WOW! AMAZING! I'VE SAILED THE SEVEN SEAS SEARCHING FOR THESE 30 PORTRAIT PEOPLE, AND NOW THAT OUR JOURNEY IS ALMOST OVER, I JUST HOPE THE PIRATES DON'T MAKE THEM WALK THE PLANK! I'M SURE THOSE FARAWAY CASTAWAYS WOULD PREFER TO BE MAROONED ON A DESERT ISLAND THAN TO MEET THESE BARMY BUCCANEERS. ALL HANDS ON DECK!

EXHIBIT 12 – THE GREAT PORTRAIT EXHIBITION

OUR JOURNEY IS NOW OVER, PORTRAIT PERUSERS, BUT WHAT A FITTING FINALE: A FANTASTIC EXHIBITION IN A PROPER ART GALLERY. WOW! AMAZING! THE CROWD HERE SEEMS MUCH MORE WELCOMING THAN ODLAW'S ODD ENSEMBLE. I'M ALSO REALLY PLEASED THAT ALL 30 OF THE CHARACTERS WE'VE BEEN HUNTING FOR ARE HERE AMONGST THE GALLERY GAZERS. SEE IF YOU CAN SPOT THEM AS THEY WANDER FREELY AMONG THE VISITORS ENJOYING THE SHOW. I HOPE YOU FOUND THEM IN THE PREVIOUS PAGES, TOO. IF NOT, THERE'S STILL PLENTY OF TIME TO DO SO – THE EXHIBITION NEVER CLOSES. HAPPY HUNTING!

WHERE'S WALLY?

THE GREAT PICTURE HUNT!

CHECKLISTS & ANSWERS

Lots more things for Wally watchers to look for!

EXHIBIT 1 – ODLAW'S PICTURE PANDEMONIUM

- A green-skinned pirate
- Two ghost imposters
- Five mummies
- A bandaged finger
- Two spiders
- A head and crossbones
- A drooping flower
- Two teddy tattoos
- A black cat
- The sun
- Eight stripy witches' hats
- Fourteen ladders
- Twelve vultures
- Upside-down skull and crossbones
- Four flying witches
- A pair of heart-shaped sunglasses
- Three spike-topped helmets
- A puzzled, fangless vampire
- A drinking straw
- A squashed Viking

EXHIBIT 2 – A SPORTING LIFE

- Hitting a hole-in-one
- A centaur circle
- A volleyball court
- Serving an Ace
- A boxer saved by the belle
- Four under Pa
- The baseball batter's swing
- A pool table
- A Jim instructor
- Dancers at a soccer ball
- Team subs
- A marshal arts class
- Weightlifters pumping iron
- Shadow boxers
- A football quarterback
- Snow-peaked caps
- A pair of swimming trunks
- An archer with a long bow
- A steeple chase
- Pear skating

SPOT THE DIFFERENCE

EXHIBIT 4 – BROWN SAILORS & GREEN SCALERS AGAIN

DID YOU SPOT THESE?

- A missing tail-end
- An absent cloud
- A brown balloon
- A balloon number missing
- A missing tooth
- A missing lasso
- Some missing smoke
- A missing flag
- A monster without spots
- A back-to-front number
- A missing flag number
- A missing monster
- An absent sailor
- A missing telescope
- A man with a yellow beard
- Some missing green slime
- An extra sailor
- A slime gun without a nozzle
- A brown sea-creature
- A sailor in a white top

EXHIBIT 5 – THE PINK PARADISE PARTY

- Two skate on skates
- Drainpipe trousers
- A heavy-metal guitarist
- Two mixing desks
- A pencil skirt
- Ball room dancers
- Two bugs jitterbugging
- A sole singer
- Oxford bags
- A Mini skirt
- A tea shirt
- Two fox trotters
- Platform shoes
- Some disc jockeys
- Oliver Twisting
- A Duke box and jukebox
- Dancing the knight away
- Beehive hairdos
- Squares square-dancing
- Two door men